T0198518

around wales ROUTE 650

by

Sior Roberts

Supporting The South Wales
Multiple Sclerosis Therapy Centre
Swansea

2020

AuthorHouse™ UK
1663 Liberty Drive
Bloomington, IN 47403 USA
www.authorhouse.co.uk
Phone: 0800 047 8203 (Domestic TFN)
+44 1908 723714 (International)

This book is printed on acid-free paper.

ISBN: 978-1-7283-5194-0 (sc)
ISBN: 978-1-7283-5193-3 (e)

Print information available on the last page.

Published by AuthorHouse 04/15/2020

authorHOUSE®

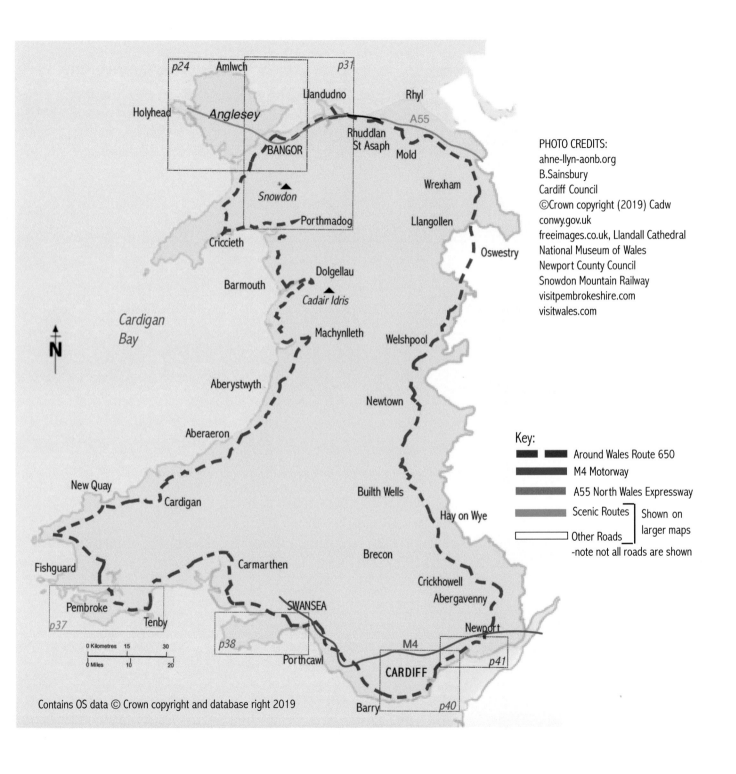

p24

Amlwch

p31

Holyhead

Anglesey

Llandudno

Rhyl

A55

BANGOR

Rhuddlan
St Asaph

Mold

Snowdon

Wrexham

Porthmadog

Llangollen

Criccieth

Oswestry

Barmouth

Dolgellau

Cadair Idris

Welshpool

*Cardigan
Bay*

Machynlleth

N

Aberystwyth

Newtown

Aberaeron

New Quay

Cardigan

Builth Wells

Hay on Wye

Fishguard

Brecon

Crickhowell

Pembroke

Carmarthen

Abergavenny

p37

Tenby

SWANSEA

Newport

p38

M4

0 Kilometres   15   30

Porthcawl

p41

0 Miles   10   20

CARDIFF

p40

Contains OS data © Crown copyright and database right 2019

Barry

PHOTO CREDITS:
ahne-llyn-aonb.org
B.Sainsbury
Cardiff Council
©Crown copyright (2019) Cadw
conwy.gov.uk
freeimages.co.uk, Llandall Cathedral
National Museum of Wales
Newport County Council
Snowdon Mountain Railway
visitpembrokeshire.com
visitwales.com

Key:

▬ ▬ ▬ Around Wales Route 650
▬▬▬ M4 Motorway
▬▬▬ A55 North Wales Expressway
▬▬▬ Scenic Routes   Shown on
                            larger maps
☐ Other Roads
-note not all roads are shown

**FROM
MOUNTAINS**

Snowdon Range, North Wales

**TO
LAKES**

Trefeglwys, Mid Wales

**TO THE
SEA**

Three Cliffs Bay, Gower, South Wales

A BRIEF TIMELINE OF WELSH HISTORY

4,000 BC Farming is introduced into Wales

2,000 BC Bronze is introduced into Wales

1,000 BC Hill forts built during the Iron Age

600 BC The Celts settle in Wales

50 AD The Romans begin the conquest of Wales

78 AD The Romans conquered Wales

407 The Roman army leaves Britain. Afterwards Wales splits into separate kingdoms.

856 Rhodri Mawr defeats the Danes

1040 First Prince of Wales, Gruffydd ap Llywelyn secured borders

1063 English invaded: Gruffydd ap Llywelyn killed

1066 Normand invaded: King Harold of England killed.

1215 Magna Carta signed

1255 Llewellyn becomes king of Gwynedd

1267 Henry III of England makes the Treaty of Montgomery with Llewellyn

1277 Llewellyn is forced to submit to the English king Edward I

1282 The Welsh rebel

1283 The rebellion is crushed

1294 The Welsh rebel again

1295 The rebellion is crushed

1301 Edward makes his son, also called Edward, Prince of Wales

1400 Owain Glyndwr leads another rebellion

1413 The rebellion ends

1485 Henry Tudor lands at Milford Haven

1536 The Act of Union reforms Welsh government

1563 Bible published in Welsh Language

1642 During the Civil War Wales supports the king

1647 Harlech Castle falls to parliamentary forces

1750 The Industrial Revolution begins to transform Wales

1800 First of great Welsh canals built

1839 The Rebecca Riots occurred, toll gate destroyed in protest against high fees

1850's Coal fields in South Wales developed

1900-03 Strike at Penrhyn Quarry; longest labour dispute in history; 3000 workers walked out

1913 Explosion at Senghenydd's pit killed 439 miners

1916 Lloyd George first Welshman to become British prime minister

1955 Cardiff became capital of Wales

1966 Slag pile collapsed at school in Aberfan, 144 children and teachers killed

1969 Investiture of Charles as Prince of Wales

1984 Year-long miner's strike virtually ended coal industry in the country

1999 The Welsh Assembly opens

2005 Charles, Prince of Wales married Camilla Parker Bowles

2008 Tower Colliery, last deep mine in Wales closed

2011 Prince William of Wales married Catherine Middleton

Welcome to "Around Wales Route 650"

The Route (shown dotted red on the map) starts and finishes in Cardiff, the capital of Wales and follows, in an anti-clockwise direction, the Wales - England border (including a short length of highway in England), the main coastal strips of North, West and South Wales.

However, the Route can be joined at any point depending on your arrival in Wales be it by air, sea, road or rail. The total length of the route, including those shown around scenic areas is some 650 miles.

Two major highways traverse east - west; the A55 Expressway in the north from the border to Holyhead in the west and the M4 Motorway in the south which extends westwards, again from the border, to beyond Swansea.

There are no 'high-speed road links' running north-south but a large network of various class of road exists across the country. Some of the major ones are shown in white on the main map. Wales has many interesting and picturesque locations inland and routes to some of these, which are not too far off the Around Wales Route 650, are shown in orange.

ITINERARIES

The picturesque Coastal route allows several ways of plotting your itinerary. The 6 day tour lays out a route, splitting each day into manageable distances and taking in some of the major highlights. The other 4 itineraries, Anglesey, Snowdonia, South Pembrokeshire and the Gower Peninsula have been drawn up for those with a specific interest, whether it be sea scape, mountains, National Parks or designated Areas of Outstanding Natural Beauty and so will take additional time to explore.

DAY 1- Cardiff - Newtown approx 109mls

DAY 2- Newtown - LLandudno approx 92mls

DAY 3- Llandudno - Barmouth approx 83mls

DAY 4- Barmouth - Fishguard. approx 99mls

DAY 5- Fishguard - Swansea. approx 95mls

DAY 6- Swansea - Cardiff. approx 52mls

INSET MAPS

CARDIFF was granted city status in 1905 and recognised as the capital of Wales in 1955. It is Wales' largest city and the eleventh-largest city in the UK. A significant tourist centre and the most popular visitor destination in Wales.

The Romans invaded Wales about 50 AD and built a fort on the site of Cardiff castle. When the Normans conquered Glamorgan Robert Fitz Hammon built a wooden castle within the walls of the old Roman fort which was rebuilt in stone in the early 12th century. The town grew up in the shadow of the castle. Owen Glendower burnt Cardiff down in 1404 but it was rebuilt quickly as the buildings were of wood and thatched roofs. During the 15th, 16th and 17th centuries it was a small thriving port town trading with France and the Channel Islands as well as other British ports. The town grew rapidly from the 1830s onwards with the building of a dock, and Cardiff became the main port for exports of coal from the valleys. Its status as a major town came when the site of the University College South Wales and Monmouthshire was chosen in 1893.

In 1877 a permanent military presence was established in the town with the completion of Maindy Barracks.

More on Cardiff page 24, 25 and 40.

Starting the journey we leave Cardiff & head eastwards to the A48 towards Newport >>

DAY 1 Cardiff to Newtown

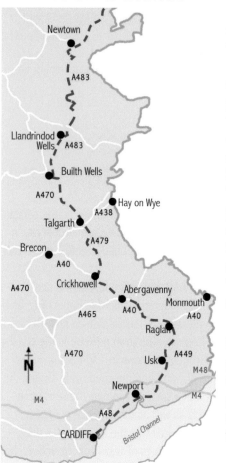

NEWPORT

lies some12 miles north-east of Cardiff and was granted city
status in 2002. It lies on the River Usk close to its confluence
with the Severn Estuary and is the third largest city in Wales.
Newport has long been a port and became the focus of coal
exports from the eastern South Wales Valleys. Industry was expanding on the east side of the river with most of the population based on the west side which meant a 4 mile walk to
cross the river by the town bridge. Although a ferry operated,
due to the tide's changing times and its extreme rise and fall,
it was impractical as a means of getting to work.

This prompted the construction of the now famous Transporter Bridge as a more economical solution than tunnelling
under the river or the building of a bridge which would allow
the passage of the tall ships of the era. The bridge was opened in 1906. It is only one of
six Transporter Bridges still in use.

You can get a different perspective of Newport from high up from the top of this Edwardian Transporter Bridge.

Belle Vue Park's features are typical of a Victorian public park, including conservatories,
pavilion, bandstand and rockeries. The Park also contains a number of rare specimens -
the Himalayan Magnolias and Judas Trees blossom in May. In June and July the Tulip Tree
produces its distinctive orange tulip-shaped flowers and Autumn brings glorious leaf
colour including the clear yellow leaves of Ginko Biloba and the glorious crimson leaves of
the Liquidambar. Entry to the Park is free but car parking charges apply.

See pages 40 & 41 for larger scale road maps
for Cardiff & Newport

RAGLAN

stands at the crossing point of two Roman roads Gloucester to Usk and Chepstow to Abergavenny. Markets were held in the town from the mid 1300's and the market cross, a massive base on which a lamp post has been mounted, stands in the centre of the cross roads. The base of the cross formed the table on which bargains were struck.

In the late 14th century Raglan Castle was probably no more than a hill fort but early in the 15th it was greatly expanded. The castle ruins became neglected and were used as a quarry for those needing stone to repair their houses. Dressed stones can be seen in local farmhouses and cottages. The railway station buildings, following its closure in 1955, have been moved to St. Fagans Museum near Cardiff.

MONMOUTH

"Town on the Monnow", the historic county town of Monmouthshire where the River Monnow joins the River Wye, 2 miles from the border with England. The town was the site of a small Roman fort and became established after the Normans built a castle here. Its medieval stone gated bridge is the only one of its type remaining in Britain. The castle built in 1067 was the birthplace of King Henry V. By the end of the 18th century, the town had become a popular centre for visitors undertaking the "Wye Tour", an excursion by boat through the scenic Wye Valley

CRICKHOWELL

Notable features include three churches, the seventeenth-century stone bridge over the River Usk (with its odd arches, twelve on one side, thirteen on the other, and its seat built into the walls, the 14th-century parish church of St Edmund, and the ruins of Crickhowell Castle on the green "tump" beside the A40 road.

Crickhowell's Market Hall (originally the Town Hall) on The Square dates from 1834, nowadays there are market stalls on the ground floor and a cafe on the first floor old courtroom. The stone building, raised on twin doric columns, is Grade II listed. The popular Green Man Festival is held here in August.

TALGARTH

Talgarth Church

This small market town has notable buildings including its 14th Century parish church and 13th Century Pele Tower located in the town centre.

ABERGAVENNY

The market held on Tuesday, Friday and Saturday has long been the focus of trade through the town. Tradesmen sell all kinds of goods from locally grown produce to various crafted articles. The once livestock market which had been active for over 150 years closed in 2013 and has now moved to Bryngwyn near Raglan.

Brecon Beacons National Park established in 1957 includes Pen y Fan, South Wales' highest mountain at 2907 ft. The Brecon Beacons are believed to be named after the ancient practice of lighting beacons on mountains to warn of attacks by invaders. They are used for training members of the UK armed forces and military reservists. One of the starting points for walkers up Pen y Fan is on the A470 known as Storey Arms, now an outdoor training centre.

HAY ON WYE

A small market town on the Welsh side of the Wales/England border is known for its bookshops and the venue for the annual Hay Literary Festival since 1988. The Festival draws thousands of visitors over a ten day period at the end of May / beginning of June, when big literary names from all over the world attend and give talks.

LLANDRINDOD WELLS

The Roman occupation of Britain provides the first evidence of spa waters in the area and still provides health-giving waters for visitors today. The Roman settlement at Castell Collen, just outside Llandrindod Wells is an important archaeological site. There are many regular attractions to cater for visitors including the Drama Festival Week at the beginning of May each year and the Victorian Festival at the end of August.

NEWTOWN

Was founded as a market town at the end of the 13th century. The town's connection with the textile industry was revived in the 20th century when businesswoman Laura Ashley established her home furnishing and clothing empire in the area. Nearby is a wealth of castles and country houses including Powys Castle & Gardens in Welshpool, Montgomery Castle, Dolforwyn Castle, Gregynog Hall & Gardens and Glansevern Hall & Gardens. A number of small local museums & galleries can be found in the centre of town. Newtown offers a variety of accommodation from hotels, lodges, cottages, b&b's and provides the ideal base to explore the surrounding area.

BRECON

Market town lies within the Brecon Beacons National Park. The Norman castle overlooking the town was built in the late 11th century. The town walls are built of cobble with four gatehouses. Today only fragments survive and these are protected as scheduled monuments. Saint Mary's church was built in 1510; the tower has eight bells which have been rung since 1750. It is a Grade II* listed building. Plough Lane Chapel in Lion Street is also a Grade II* listed building and dates back to 1841

BUILTH WELLS

A pretty town and a delight to explore. The Wyeside Arts Centre on Castle Street was built as a market hall and Assembly Rooms during Builth's heyday as a Spa town. The first record of mineral waters at Builth comes from 1740, but it was not until further developments that Builth gained a reputation as a Spa town. Strand Hall, is a historic building, built in neoclassical style as a market hall with an exterior of red and yellow bricks. A Grade II listed pillar box in front of the Arts Centre dates back to the reign of George VI and on nearby West Street stands a pillar box which dates back to the reign of Queen Victoria. There are 43 listed buildings in Builth. The Groe is a life-sized sculpture of a black bull, a reminder of the origins of Builth Wells. The Royal Welsh Show, the largest agricultural show in the UK, is held here in July each year.

DAY 2 Newtown to Llandudno

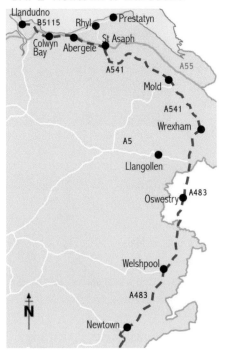

WELSHPOOL

A major attraction to Welshpool is the Monday Cattle Market, believed to be one of the largest one-day markets in the Europe. The Welshpool Carnival takes place in May.

The restored octagonal cockpit in the centre of the town is unusual being the only one in Wales on its original site.

The Welshpool & Llanfair Light Railway - a narrow gauge steam train, was originally built to take local people to market with their sheep and cattle, operates throughout the summer months between Easter and early October.

WREXHAM

The largest town in north Wales and an administrative, commercial, retail and educational centre. The Monday market is the largest in North Wales. It is a very popular town to visit being a short drive away from a number of historical sites.

MOLD Mold Castle, on Bailey Hill in the town is a motte-and-bailey castle erected around 1072. St Mary's Church, is an Anglican church and a Grade I listed building.

The Mold Food & Drink Festival is held each September. The food festival has a main event area on the edge of the town centre

The nearby Pontcysyllte Aqueduct built over two hundred years ago to ferry raw materials and finished products in and out of the area. The arches reach a height of 200ft as they span the river. One can walk or ride in a canal boat along its entire length. In the summer months you can travel over the canal as you dine on a canal boat.

LLANGOLLEN

One of the UNESCO World Heritage Sites with something for every visitor, is renowned for the surrounding hills and River Dee and the nearby Valle Crucis Abbey. It is also noted for hosting the International Eisteddfod held annually in July when the town is awash with colour with the many contestants parading the streets in their national costumes.

RHUDDLAN Castle was erected by Edward I in 1277 but was not completed until 1282. It was King Edward I of England's temporarily residence, and his daughter, Elizabeth, is presumed to have been born there.

St ASAPH

This beautiful Cathedral was built around 1150 and enlarged to its present size by 1400. Its appearance, like a castle, is thought to be because it was built by Edward's castle builders.

BODELWYDDAN is well known for its "Marble Church". The Church was consecrated in 1860. It is open daily from 09:30 to 16:30 throughout the year except from Christmas Day until January 6th. St. Margaret's is one of Britain's finest Victorian Churches and its interior is decorated with a variety of marble.

COLWYN BAY Is a seaside resort with its long Promenade following the vast sweep from Old Colwyn to Penrhyn Bay. Another attraction is the Welsh Mountain Zoo. with many rare and endangered species from around the world including snow leopards, red pandas, Sumatran tigers, chimpanzees and Californian sea lions.

LLANDUDNO. is a classic Victorian seaside resort with a pier, Punch and Judy show, Donkey Man and Alice in Wonderland. Travel up to summit of the Great Orme either by car, train or in a cable car where you'll be rewarded with incredible views of its surrounding mountains and coastal towns.

Great Orme

DAY 3 Llandudno to Barmouth

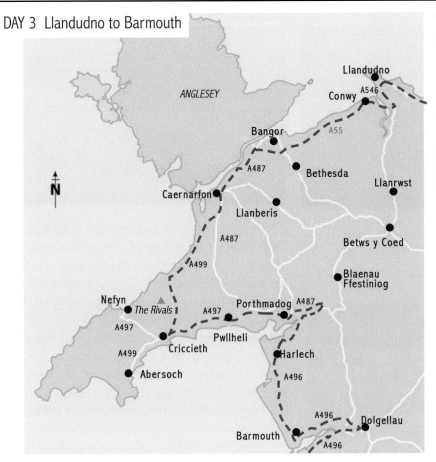

CONWY

A town with a mighty 13th-century castle and town walls. It is considered by UNESCO to be one of "the finest examples of late 13th century/early 14th century military architecture in Europe" and is classed as a World Heritage site.

The Quay offers a number of amenities where you can find the smallest house in Great Britain and also enjoy a refreshing drink outside or in a cosy quayside pub. Conwy also offers a whole host of places to eat and drink from fine dining restaurants, traditional pubs and snug cafes as well as a number of hotels and B&Bs. Local boat tours are available at the Quay.

BANGOR,

a university city, is the oldest city in Wales, one of the smallest cities in the United Kingdom and one of only six places classed as a city in Wales. Another claim to fame is that Bangor allegedly has the longest High Street in Wales and the United Kingdom.

CAERNARFON

Garth Pier is the second longest pier in Wales, and the ninth longest in the British Isles, at 1,500 feet in length. It was opened in 1893 and was a promenade pier. It was listed to be "the best in Britain of the older type of pier without a large pavilion at the landward end".

Bangor Cathedral - the Cathedral Church of St Deiniol is a Grade I Listed building and is set in a sloping oval churchyard. The site has been used for Christian worship since the sixth century but the present building dates from the twelfth century. It has a two-bay chancel, transepts, a crossing tower, a seven-bay nave and a tower at the west end. While the building it-

self is not the oldest, and certainly not the biggest, the bishopric of Bangor is one of the oldest in the UK.

A Royal town lying on the southern bank of the Menai Strait facing the Isle of Anglesey. The present castle building was constructed between 1283 and 1330. It is open to the public and includes the regimental museum of the Royal Welch Fusiliers. The investiture ceremony for Charles, Prince of Wales was held at the Castle in1969.

Caernarfon town walls form a complete circuit around the old town, However, only a small section is accessible to the public. The town walls and castle are part of a World Heritage Site and claimed to be "the finest examples of late 13th century and early 14th century military architecture in Europe".

The oldest public house in Caernarfon is the Black Boy Inn, which has stood inside the town walls since the 16th century, and many people claim to have seen ghosts within the building. The Old Market Hall is a Grade II listed building now a pub and music venue.

A market is held every Saturday throughout the year and also on Mondays in the Summer.

The statue of David Lloyd George in Castle Square was erected in 1921 when Lloyd George was Prime Minister. He is buried in Llanystymdwy near Porthmadog.

Caernarfon Airport is 4.5 miles to the south west. It has an aviation museum and offers pleasure flights.

In 1956, a large part of the Llŷn Peninsula was designated an Area of Outstanding Natural Beauty under the National Parks and Access to the Countryside Act 1949.

PORTHMADOG

The small Welsh coastal town developed in the 19th century after William Madocks built a sea wall, "the Cob", in 1810 to reclaim a large proportion of the beach from the sea for agricultural use. Porthmadog became a flourishing port for exporting slate as the rapidly expanding cities of England needed high quality roofing slate. The slate was transported to the new port by tramway from the quarries in Ffestiniog and Llanfrothen. However, since the decline of the slate industry Porthmadog has become a shopping centre and tourist destination. It is the terminus of the Ffestiniog Railway.

Portmeirion is a tourist village off the A487. It was designed and built by Sir Clough Williams-Ellis between 1925 and 1975 in the style of an Italian village, and is now owned by a charitable trust.

CRICCIETH

The building of the castle began in about 1230 and some 30 years later its size doubled with the addition of another wall and tower. In the early 13th Century Criccieth was little more than a church and a few houses beside the newly erected castle. In 1282 Edward I repaired the castle and built a chain of castles having conquered the land.

HARLECH

Harlech castle is a Grade I listed medieval fortification built by Edward I during his invasion of Wales. During the Wars of the Roses Harlech was held by the Lancastrians for seven years, before Yorkist troops forced its surrender. In 1642, following the outbreak of the English Civil War, the castle was held by forces loyal to Charles I, holding out until 1647 when it became the last fortification to surrender to the Parliamentary armies. The castle is now managed by Cadw, the Welsh Government's historic environment service, as a tourist attraction.

Along with other castles in Wales UNESCO considers Harlech to be one of "the finest examples of late 13th century and early 14th century military architecture in Europe", it is classed as a World Heritage site. The castle built of local stone is of concentric design, featuring a massive gatehouse that probably once provided high-status accommodation for the castle constable and visiting dignitaries. The sea originally came much closer to Harlech and a water-gate and a long flight of steps leads down from the castle to the former shore. This allowed the castle to be resupplied by sea during sieges.

Harlech is reputedly to have one of the steepest roads in the world.

BARMOUTH

was once a shipbuilding town and more recently has become a seaside resort. Buildings of interest include the medieval Ty Gwyn tower house, the 19th century Ty Crwn roundhouse prison and St John's Church. William Wordsworth, a visitor to Barmouth in the 19th century, described it thus: "With a fine sea view in front, the mountains behind, the glorious estuary running eight miles inland, and Cadair Idris within compass of a day's walk, Barmouth can always hold its own against any rival".

The busy harbour plays host to the annual Three Peaks yacht race.

The Barmouth Ferry sails from Barmouth to Penrhyn Point, where it connects with the narrow gauge Fairbourne Railway for the village of Fairbourne.

Barmouth Bridge, which takes the Cambrian Line over the River Mawddach.

DAY 4 Barmouth to Fishguard

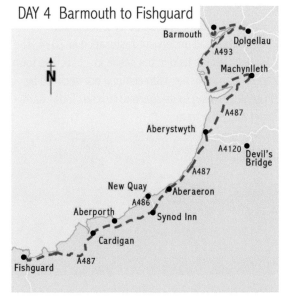

DEVIL'S BRIDGE

The village is best known for the bridge that spans the Afon Mynach. The bridge is unusual in that three separate bridges are coexistent, each one built upon the previous bridge: the earlier ones were not demolished The unique Devils Bridge Falls is a world famous tourist attraction 12 miles east of Aberystwyth on the A4120.

ABERYSTWYTH

An ancient market town and holiday resort. The seafront boasts the oldest pier in Wales, built in 1864. The best vantage point is at the end of north beach's promenade atop Constitution Hill where you'll also find the world's largest Camera Obscura which provides a bird's eye view of over 1000 square miles. The Camera Obscura is accessible via the Cliff Railway which is the longest cliff railway in Britain. Aberystwyth is also a major Welsh educational centre the university college established in 1872 and houses the National Library of Wales.

ABERAERON

was developed from 1805 and the harbour operated as a port and supported a shipbuilding industry in the 19th century. Steam ships continued to visit the harbour until the 1920's; it is now a small half-tide harbour for recreational craft. The town is notable for the sale of honey and honey by-products.
An annual festival of Welsh ponies and cobs is held every August and the annual carnival takes place on August Bank Holiday Monday.

NEW QUAY

a beautiful fishing village with its picturesque harbour and sandy beach and trips from the harbour to see the bottle nose dolphins. Porpoise and Atlantic Grey seals can be viewed in the bay during certain times of the year. The New Quay Honey Farm, the largest bee farm in Wales is also a popular attraction. The annual Cardigan Bay Regatta which has been a feature in the area since before 1870 usually takes place in August.

FISHGUARD

consists of two parts, Lower Fishguard and the "Main Town". The main town, with the Parish church and shops, which lies upon the hill, is joined by a steep and winding road to the south of Lower Fishguard.
Lower Fishguard is believed to be the site of the original hamlet from which modern Fishguard has grown. It is in a deep valley where the River Gwaun flows and is a typical fishing village with a short tidal quay.

CARDIGAN

was developed around the Norman castle built in the late 11th/early 12th century and underwent restoration in 2014. The first National Eisteddfod was held in the castle in 1176. The town became an important port in the 18th century, but declined by the early 20th century owing to its shallow harbour. Today Cardigan is a compact and busy town.

NEWPORT is a popular tourist destination was founded in about 1197 and was a busy port founded primarily on the growing medieval wool trade. Newport Castle is situated on a spur which overlooks the town and much of the surrounding countryside. Though in ruins since at least the 17th century, a house incorporating the castle walls is still inhabited. There is, in the town a significant mediaeval pottery kiln from the 15th century, believed to be the only intact example in Britain.

ST DAVIDS

was given city status in the 16th century and is the UK's smallest city in terms of population and urban area. It is the final resting place of Saint David, Wales's patron saint, and named after him. In addition to the cathedral, interesting features include the 14th-century Tower Gate, the Celtic Old Cross and a number of art galleries.

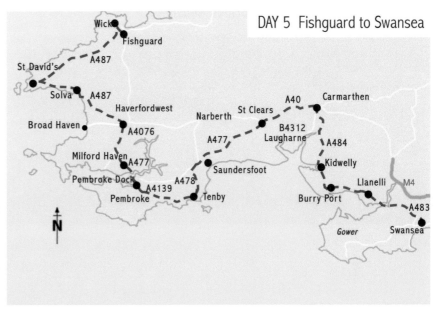

DAY 5 Fishguard to Swansea

SOLVA

boasts a bustling quay, a charming High Street with cafes, craft shops and galleries as well as easy access to beaches and walks both on the Pembrokeshire National Coast Path and inland.

Some of Pembrokeshire's Glorious Beaches

Broadhaven

Dale

Marloes Sands

HAVERFORDWEST

Haverfordwest was established almost 1,000 years ago and in olden times was the second largest port in Wales. The centre of the town is dominated by the Western Cleddau that runs through the middle of the town and by the castle, built in about 1110. Situated within the Castle wall and previously the old prison governor's house is the town museum which houses exhibitions of art and local history and has artefacts relating to the town's past. On the bank of the river are the recently excavated and repaired ruins of an Augustinian Priory. They occupy a pleasant setting beside the river, a short walk from the town centre.

PEMBROKE

Pembroke Castle, a medieval castle, stands on a site that has been occupied at least since the Roman period. It is most famous for being the birthplace of Henry VII, the founder of the Tudor Dynasty and Britain's only Welsh king. Henry VII was King of England between 1485 and 1509. It was designated a Grade I listed building in 1951, and later underwent major restoration. The castle is the largest privately-owned castle in Wales and is open to the public.

MILFORD was founded in 1793 and takes its name from the natural harbour of **MILFORD HAVEN** which has been used as a port since. It was designed to a grid pattern, and originally intended to be a whaling centre, though by 1800 it was developing as a Royal Navy dockyard and remained as such until the dockyard was transferred to Pembroke in 1814. It then became a commercial dock. By 2010, the town's port had become the fourth largest in the United Kingdom in terms of tonnage, and continues its important role in the United Kingdom's energy sector with several oil refineries and one of the biggest LNG terminals in the world.

TENBY

A 13th century medieval walled town noted for its sandy beaches. The town walls include the Five Arches, built in the 16thC following fears of a second Spanish Armada, a barbican gatehouse, Museum and Art Gallery, a 15th Century Church St. Mary's.There are 372 listed buildings and other structures in and around Tenby. The Sunday Times rated Tenby's Castle Beach the best beach in the UK in 2019.

Boats sail from Tenby's harbour to the offshore monastic Caldey Island.

SAUNDERSFOOT

A large village and a popular holiday destinations. St Issells church lies in a dell to the north of Saundersfoot and is a Grade II* listed building. The harbour was built for the export of anthracite coal from the many mines in the area, although coal was exported from the beach for centuries before this. The village grew up to serve the port which by 1837 had five jetties handling coal and iron ore and subsequently pig iron and firebricks from local sources. The industry finally faded away in the early years of the twentieth century. Saundersfoot holds its annual charitable cheese festival and New Years Day swim every year which is sponsored by local businesses with more than 1,000 people taking part.

St CLEARS

The Priory Church of St Mary Magdalene was founded in around 1100 and is considered to have the best surviving Norman stone carving in Carmarthenshire. The stained-glass windows date from about 1929 in a Grade II listed building.

The Norman St Clears Castle was constructed in the 12th century and the town grew around it. The castle mound can still be seen.

LAUGHARNE

The home of Dylan Thomas from 1949 until his death in 1953. He is buried in Laugharne churchyard, his grave marked by a white cross. There are a number of landmarks namely the Boathouse, where he lived with his family from 1949 to 1953, and is now a museum; the parish church of St Martin and the 12th-century Castle.

NARBERTH

Was founded around a Welsh court, and some time later became a Norman stronghold. The town has many art galleries; it also houses the Narberth Museum, the former town hall which still houses the cell where the leaders of the Rebecca Riots were imprisoned and a ruined castle. Narberth with its wide range of independent shops, was reported by The Guardian in 2014 as "not only a gastronomic hub for west Wales but also one of the liveliest, most likable little towns in the UK". Narberth Food Festival takes place on the fourth weekend of September every year. It features celebrity chefs, cookery demonstrations, music, entertainment as well as children's activities. Narberth Civic Week is held during the last full week of July. A parade through the town is held leading to one of the churches following which a service is held to welcome the newly appointed Mayor. Also during Civic Week various activities are arranged for children, their families and visitors to the town. The culmination of Civic Week is the annual Carnival Day Parade, a tradition which dates back over 100 years. Narberth's Winter Carnival is held in December.

Laugharne Castle

Here two giant medieval stone towers stand guard over the remains of a magnificent Tudor mansion, all set in 19th century ornamental gardens.

CARMARTHEN

Claimed to be the oldest town in Wales but little remains of the original medieval castle. The old Gatehouse still dominates Nott Square. Castle House, within the old walls, is a museum and Tourist Information Centre. St Peter's is the largest parish church in the Diocese of St David's. Built of local red sandstone and grey shale it consists of a west tower, nave, chancel, south aisle and a Consistory Court. The tower contains eight bells.

Picton's monument was erected 1828 at the west end of the town to honour Lieutenant General Sir Thomas Picton, who had died at the Battle of Waterloo in 1815.

The foundation stone was laid on Monument Hill in 1847 and some 150 years later the top section was declared to be unsafe and was taken down. Four years later, the whole monument was rebuilt stone-by-stone on stronger foundations. There are many listed buildings in the town.

LLANELLI

Historically a mining town, Llanelli grew significantly in the 18th and 19th century with the mining of coal and later the tinplate industry and steelworks. With the decline in these, Llanelli is now a leisure and tourism destination, with many new developments such as the new Llanelli Scarlets rugby stadium, the Old Castle Works leisure village and a National Hunt racecourse at nearby Ffos Las.

Local attractions include the Millennium Coastal Path, the National Wetlands Centre, about 1-mile to the east of Llanelli. Llanelly House is one of Llanelli's most historic properties, an example of an early 18th-century Georgian town house, Parc Howard Museum set in the grounds of Parc Howard, St Elli's Parish Church is a Grade II* listed building.

Machynys Ponds, a Site of Special Scientific Interest notable for its dragonfly population, is 1 mile to the south of Llanelli.

KIDWELLY

was used as a location for the film Monty Python and the Holy Grail. The castle consists of a square inner bailey defended by four round towers, which overlook a semi-circular outer curtain wall on the landward side, with the massive gatehouse next to the river. The castle is relatively well-preserved, and is managed by Cadw.

BURRY PORT

lies on the Loughor estuary with its harbour looking south towards the picturesque Gower peninsula. In 1832 a harbour was built at Burry Port and the town developed around 1850. The harbour is now a marina for small leisure craft. The Pembrey Burrows sand dune and wetland system and the Cefn Sidan sands lie nearby. The town has a proud musical heritage. Burry Port is where Amelia Earhart landed as the first woman to fly across the Atlantic Ocean.

The National Botanic Garden of Wales is both a visitor attraction and a centre for botanical research and conservation, and features the world's largest single-span glasshouse. It is situated off the A48 east of Carmarthen.

SWANSEA

was granted city status in 1969 to mark Prince Charles's investiture as the Prince of Wales. It is the second largest city in Wales. Within the city centre are: ruins of the castle, National Waterfront Museum, Glynn Vivian Art Gallery, Swansea Museum, Dylan Thomas Centre, and the Market, which is the largest covered market in Wales.

During the 19th-century industrial heyday, Swansea was the key centre of the copper-smelting industry. The port of Swansea initially traded in wine, hides, wool, cloth and later in coal.

Brangwyn Hall is a multi-use venue and hosts a Festival of Music and the Arts. The city has three Grade One listed buildings namely Swansea Castle, the Tabernacle Chapel, Morriston and the Guildhall with its white Portland stone and a tall clock-tower which makes it a landmark. There are also a number of Grade II* listed buildings in the City. The Victorian Grand Theatre celebrated its centenary in 1997.

The poet Dylan Thomas was born in the town and lived here for 23 years. His take on Swansea was that it was an "ugly lovely town".
A bronze statue of Dylan Thomas stands in the Maritime Quarter.

Swansea City A.F.C. and the Ospreys Rugby Football Club is are based at the Liberty Stadium situated north of the City. St Helens Rugby and Cricket Ground is the home of Swansea RFC and Glamorgan County Cricket Club have previously played matches there. On this ground, Sir Garfield Sobers hit six sixes in one over; the first time this was achieved in a game of first-class cricket.

The Norwegian Church is a Grade II listed building in the docklands area of the city. built as a place of worship for Norwegian sailors when they visited the UK. It was relocated from Newport to Swansea in 1910. Swansea University has a campus in Singleton Park and opened a new Bay Campus situated in the Jersey Marine area of Swansea. Other establishments for further and higher education in the city include University of Wales Trinity Saint David and Gower College Swansea. Swansea Airport is a minor aerodrome situated on Gower providing recreational flights only.

Swansea Castle

The National Waterfront Museum
is a museum forming part of the Museum Wales and deals with Wales' history of industrial revolution and innovation.

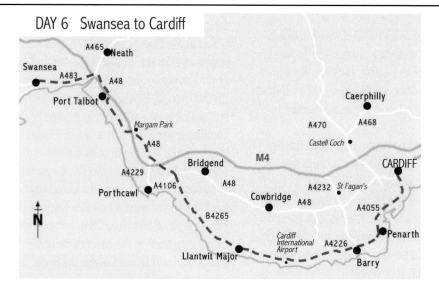

DAY 6   Swansea to Cardiff

Neath A465
Swansea A483 A48
Port Talbot
Caerphilly
Margam Park
A470 A468
A48
Castell Coch
M4
Bridgend
A4229
Porthcawl A4106
A48
CARDIFF
A4232 St Fagan's
Cowbridge A48
A4055
B4265
Penarth
Cardiff
International
Airport A4226
Llantwit Major
Barry

N

PORT TALBOT

is best known for its steelworks, one of the biggest in the world. The local beach, Aberafan Sands, is situated along the edge of the bay. In 1970 a new deep-water harbour was opened by Queen Elizabeth II and the Duke of Edinburgh.

Margam Country Park is situated about 2 miles from the town and within the park are three notable buildings: Margam Abbey, a Cistercian monastery; Margam Castle, a neo-Gothic country house and the 18th-century Orangery. The remains of a Chain Home Low early warning radar station, designed to guard against enemy surface craft and submarines in the Bristol Channel, are situated in the Park. The estate is noted for its peacock population. Also on the estate are deer, first introduced by the Romans, Aviaries on the estate house a number of rescued birds of prey. The rare breed, Glamorgan cattle, are raised on the estate. A narrow gauge train conducts visitors around the grounds in the summer. Events on the estate are held through the summer ranging from fairs selling particular goods to car rallies. The Margam Country Show is held in August.

Access is free but there is a charge for car parking and for some events.

NEATH

A settlement since Romans times, it was a market town that expanded in the 18th century with the iron, steel and tinplate industries. Coal was mined extensively in the surrounding valleys and the construction of canals and railways made Neath a major transportation hub. The River Neath is a navigable estuary and Neath was a river port until recent times. The ruins of the Cistercian Neath Abbey, now in the care of Cadw, was once the largest abbey in Wales and substantial ruins can still be seen.

BRIDGEND

has greatly expanded in size since the early 1980s and is undergoing a redevelopment project, with the town centre mainly pedestrianised. Several prehistoric burial mounds have been found in the vicinity of Bridgend, suggesting that the area was settled before Roman times. A Roman road known locally as the 'Golden Mile' is believed to be where Roman soldiers were lined up to be paid. Three castles, Coity, Newcastle, and Ogmore provided a "defensive triangle" for the area.

COWBRIDGE

lies on the site of a Roman settlement and alongside a Roman road. The  town centre is still arranged on its medieval plan, with one long street containing a number of Georgian houses. It is one of very few medieval walled towns in Wales, and substantial portions of the walls, together with the south gate, are still standing. The present Cowbridge Town Hall, served as a prison until 1830, when it was converted into a Town Hall. Eight of the original prison cells are still intact, six of which house the exhibits of Cowbridge Museum with the remainder of the building used by the town council and for public events. The Carnes' town house is a Grade 2* listed property of Medieval origin.

The town hosts the annual Cowbridge Food and Drink Festival which currently takes place in late spring. Many of the town's inns hold beer, ale and cider events. The Cowbridge Music Festival takes place every autumn in various venues throughout the town.

LLANTWIT MAJOR

has been inhabited for over 3000 years and archaeological evidence shows that it was occupied in Neolithic times. It still retains its narrow winding streets, high walls, old town hall and gatehouse, and several inns and houses dated to the 16th century. In the beach area are the remains of an Iron Age fort.

BARRY

was a village with a port and its own church and watermill. It grew when it was developed as a coal port in the 1880s. The coal trade was growing faster than the facilities at Tiger Bay in Cardiff could handle so the docks at Barry were constructed and opened in 1889 to be followed by two other docks and extensive port installations. By 1913 Barry was the largest coal exporting port in the world. Whitehouse Cottage, the oldest existing inhabited house in modern Barry, dates from the late 1500s with the east end of the building added in around 1600. It overlooks the sea at Cold Knap.

Barry Island peninsula was an island until the 1880s when it was linked to the mainland as the town of Barry expanded. Barry Island is now known for its beach and Barry Island Pleasure Park also the location of the popular TV series Gavin & Stacey.

PENARTH

area has a history of human inhabitation dating back at least 5000 years. Much later, streets of terraced houses with corner shops and public houses with local grey limestone were built giving a particular character to the town's older buildings. Penarth earned its wide reputation as "The Garden by the Sea" because of its attractive parks, open spaces and beach. A substantial part of the town has been designated as a Conservation Area because of its Victorian/Edwardian architecture. Penarth Pier, 750 feet long, was opened in 1895, and following damage caused by collision by ships the pier was rebuilt, strengthened, refurbished and revamped to be re-opened as a major tourist attraction in the Autumn of 2013.

CARDIFF

Most famously the buildings in Cathays Park, in the centre of the city are:-
1) City Hall. 2) National Museum of Wales.
3) Welsh National War Memorial. 4) University of Wales Registry Building all of which are built of Portland stone imported from Dorset.

Since the 1980s, Cardiff has seen major development and from 2000, there has been a significant change of scale of buildings both in the city centre and Cardiff Bay.

A new waterfront area at Cardiff Bay contains the Senedd building (home to the Welsh Assembly(5) opened on by The Queen in 2006) and the Wales Millennium Centre arts complex (6). This redevelopment in the Bay area has transformed it into an attractive, vibrant area.

Cardiff City Hall was opened in 1906 and built as part of the Cathays Park civic centre development and is an example of the Edwardian Baroque style.

The National Museum of Wales founded in 1905: the museum has collections of archaeology, botany, fine and applied art, geology, and zoology. The art gallery houses a collection of Old Master paintings as well as other classical works.

Cardiff Bay Barrage

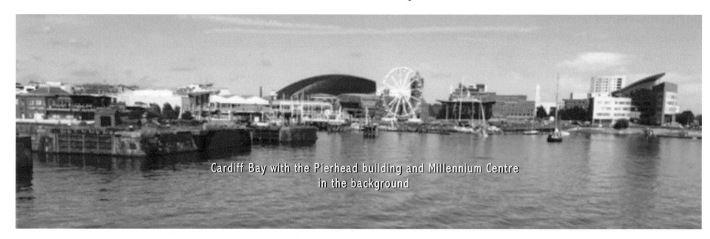

Cardiff Bay with the Pierhead building and Millennium Centre in the background

The Welsh National War Memorial was unveiled in 1928 by the then Prince of Wales and commemorates the servicemen who died during the First World War and has a plaque for those who died during the Second World War.

Millennium Centre

Cardiff Castle is a medieval castle located in the city centre. The original motte and bailey castle was built in the late 11th Century by Norman invaders on top of a 3rd century Roman fort. Further work was carried out in the second half of the 13th Century.

Roath Park Lake - The clock tower at the southern end of the Lake commemorates Captain Scott's ill-fated expedition to the South Pole; his ship the Terra Nova sailed from Cardiff in 1920.

Cardiff University, founded in 1833, was originally in Newport Road where the Applied Sciences now stand, and is now in Cathays Park.

Welsh Assembly building

Pier Head is a rich terra cotta Grade One listed building. Built in the late 1800's as offices for the Bute Dock Company.

The Principality Stadium is the national stadium of Wales and is the home of the Wales national rugby union team. It has also held Wales national football team games as well as several other major events.

St FAGANS NATIONAL MUSEUM OF HISTORY is one of world's leading open-air museums and Wales's most-visited heritage attraction. It showcases historic buildings relocated from across Wales, including a farm, a tannery, mills and a chapel.

LLANDAFF CATHEDRAL stands in the ancient city of Llandaff two miles north of Cardiff and dates from 1120. Throughout its history it has been altered, ruined and restored including the 15th Century bell tower & 19th Century Gothic architecture. Following war damage the interior was also repaired with an arch spanning the nave carrying Jacob Epstein's Aluminium Christ in Majesty.

CASTELL COCH

is a 19th-century Gothic Revival castle built above the village of Tongwynlais off the A470 north of Cardiff. The first castle on the site was built by the Normans after 1081 and the outside of the castle was rebuilt between 1875 and 1879.

Castell Coch's external features and the High Victorian interiors led it to be described as "one of the greatest Victorian triumphs of architectural composition." The surrounding beech woods contain rare plant species and unusual geological features and are protected as a Site of Special Scientific Interest.

CAERPHILLY CASTLE situated on the A469 some 8 miles north of Cardiff is the largest castle in Wales - second only to Windsor. Massive walls, towers and gatehouses were combined with sprawling water defences to cover a total of 30 acres. It was constructed in the second half of the 13th century and is famous for having introduced concentric castle defences to Britain and for its large gatehouses. It is thought that subsidence, when the water defences retreated, caused the southeast tower to lean outwards at an angle of 10 degrees as there is no evidence of deliberate destruction having been ordered. The castle is protected as a scheduled monument and as a Grade I listed building.

The following section details areas of interest adjacent or close to the Route namely:

Anglesey with its seascape, Snowdonia with its mountain scenery, South Pembrokeshire's stunning coastline and Gower Peninsula, Britain's first Area of Outstanding Natural Beauty.

Benllech Bay
Anglesey

Tryfan
Snowdonia

Dale
Pembrokeshire

Caswell Bay to Langland
Gower

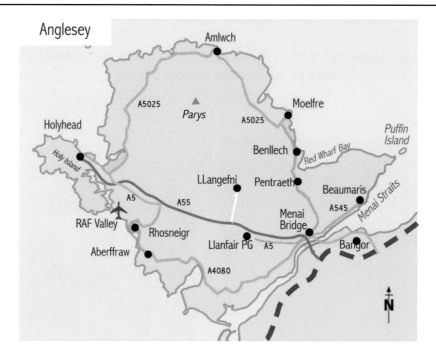

ANGLESEY has an area of 276 square miles and is by far the largest island in Wales with a population of some 70,000. Several small towns scattered around the island, make it evenly populated. It is a relatively low-lying island with the highest mountain, Holyhead Mountain, 220 metres.

There are numerous megalithic monuments and menhirs on the island. British Iron Age and Roman sites have been excavated and coins and ornaments discovered.

The rural coastline was designated an Area of Outstanding Natural Beauty in 1966. It has many sandy beaches, notably along its east coast between the towns of Beaumaris and Amlwch and the south west coast from Ynys Llanddwyn through Rhosneigr. The north coast has dramatic cliffs with small bays. The Anglesey Coastal Path around the island is 124 miles long and passes by/through 20 towns/villages.

The town of Amlwch was once largely industrialised with the important copper-mining industry at nearby Parys Mountain.

The Royal Air Force station - RAF Valley is home to the RAF Fast Jet Training School and Head Quarters of 22 Sqn Search and Rescue Helicopters, both units providing employment to about 500 civilians.

Tourism is now the major economic activity on the island. Agriculture provides the secondary source of income with local dairies being some of the most productive in the region.

Anglesey supports two of the UK's few remaining colonies of red squirrels. The RAF airstrip at Mona is a nesting site for skylarks. The sheer cliff faces at South Stack near Holyhead provide nesting sites for huge numbers of auks, including puffins, razorbills and guillemots, together with choughs and peregrine falcons. Anglesey is also home to several species of tern, including the roseate tern.

MENAI BRIDGE

designed by Thomas Telford and built by Robert Stephenson, the son of George Stephenson the famous locomotive engineer, opened in 1826 and provided the first road link between Anglesey and the mainland.

BEAUMARIS Castle was the last of the strongholds created by Edward1 in Wales. It is of near-perfect symmetry with four concentric rings of defence and included a water-filled moat and its own dock. A lack of money is believed to have resulted in its distinctive squat shape.

BENLLECH

A popular beach holiday destination. The beach has an abundance of clean yellow sand and looks out toward the Great Orme. The village has a range of hotels, camping and caravan sites and several bed and breakfasts. The Scheduled Monument Pant-Y-Saer on the outskirts of Benllech is an enclosed "hut group" monument which consists of a complex of mainly circular huts and parts of an associated substantial enclosure wall lying on a slightly elevated limestone plateau area. The monument is of national importance for its potential to enhance our knowledge of prehistoric Romano British settlement.

PENTRAETH

meaning, in Welsh, the end of or head of a beach was in 1170 the site of a battle when Hywel ab Owain Gwynedd landed with an army raised in Ireland in an attempt to claim a share of the kingdom of Gwynedd following the death of his father Owain Gwynedd. He was defeated and killed here by the forces of his half-brothers Dafydd ab Owain Gwynedd and Rhodri.

Puffin Island, just off the coast of Anglesey, is uninhabited and is designated a Site of Special Scientific Interest (SSSI) on account of its large cormorant population. Puffin Island has a breeding colony of some 40 Puffins, much less than Skomer Island off the Pembrokeshire coast. As well as the birds, there are grey seals on the island, and occasional sightings of bottlenose dolphins and harbour porpoise. It is not possible for visitors to land on the island without permission from the landowner. However if you want to see the birds then the best way is to take a boat trip around the island from Beaumaris.

RED WHARF BAY is an Area of Outstanding Natural Beauty and close to Castell Mawr Rock, believed to be the site of an Iron Age fort.

AMLWCH

The most northerly town in Wales and according to legend developed in the Middle Ages on a site that had a harbour which was not visible from the sea and so helped to reduce the chance of Viking attacks.

With the nearby copper mine, the world's biggest, at the nearby Parys Mountain, Amlwch grew rapidly in the 18th Century and was the second largest town in Wales after Merthyr Tydfil. The harbour was also extended to accommodate the ships needed to transport the ore. In the 1970s, Amlwch had an offshore single point mooring Oil Terminal which was used to receive large oil tankers which were unsuitable for the Mersey. The terminal closed in 1990. Attractions in Amlwch include its restored port area, its watch tower, maritime and copper mining museums, St Eleth's Church (dates from 1800) and the reinforced concrete Catholic church Our Lady Star of the Sea and St Winefride, built in 1937.

HOLYHEAD

is a major Irish Sea port serving Ireland and the largest town in the Isle of Anglesey. Built on Holy Island, which is separated from Anglesey by the Cymyran Strait and originally connected to Anglesey via the Four Mile Bridge and now by the Stanley Embankment.

In the mid-19th century a larger causeway was built, known locally as "The Cobb". It now carries the A5, the railway line and the A55 North Wales Expressway which runs parallel to the Cobb on a modern causeway.

South Stack on Holy Island

ABERFFRAW & LLANDDWYN

Ynys Llanddwyn is a tidal island; it remains attached to the mainland at all but the highest tides and provides views of Snowdonia and the Llŷn Peninsula.

Before leaving Anglesey don't forget to visit the small village with the longest name in Wales -

LLANFAIRPWLLGWYNGYLLGOGERYCHWYRNDROBWLLLLANTYSILIOGOGOGOCH

which translates to "Saint Mary's Church in the hollow of the white hazel near a rapid whirlpool and the Church of St. Tysilio of the red cave".

A second crossing of Menai Straits, Britannia bridge, to provide a direct rail link between London and the port of Holyhead was opened in 1850. In May 1970, the bridge was heavily damaged by fire. and the structure was subsequently rebuilt. The superstructure of the new bridge includes a lower rail deck and an upper one carrying the North Wales Expressway opened by HRH the Prince of Wales in 1980.

Snowdonia

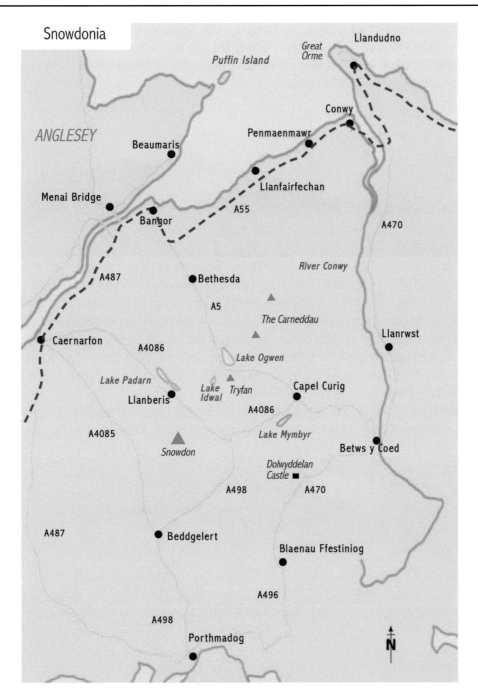

Llandudno

Great Orme

Puffin Island

ANGLESEY

Beaumaris

Conwy

Penmaenmawr

Llanfairfechan

Menai Bridge

A55

Bangor

A470

A487

River Conwy

Bethesda

A5

The Carneddau

Llanrwst

Caernarfon

A4086

Lake Ogwen

Lake Padarn

Tryfan

Capel Curig

Llanberis

Lake Idwal

A4086

A4085

Lake Mymbyr

Betws y Coed

Snowdon

Dolwyddelan Castle

A498

A470

A487

Beddgelert

Blaenau Ffestiniog

A496

A498

Porthmadog

N

SNOWDONIA is the second-largest national park in Britain and contains a wide variety of other natural features - rivers, lakes, waterfalls, forests, moorlands, glacial valleys and a picturesque coastline. The area around Snowdon is the busiest part of the park popular for climbing and walking. Snowdonia was the area where members of the first successful attempt on Mt Everest trained. Several of Wales' 'Great Little Railways' are found in Snowdonia.

BETHESDA

The town grew around the slate quarrying industries. Penrhyn Slate Quarry, Bethesda was once the largest and most productive slate quarry in the world and exported purple slate worldwide. The quarry men were suspended from ropes on the rock face and used explosives to remove large slabs of rock. The remains of inclined planes where rock was drawn up the galleries to the sheds or mills for slate processing is still evident. Part of the quarry, now modernised remains active, adjacent to the relict historic quarry. The system of benched galleries introduced here at the end of the 18th century/beginning of the 19th, is still evident along with the ropeway system (now used as an adventure zip-wire attraction and is the fastest zip wire in the world and the longest in Europe). The large tips of waste are a feature of the lower reaches of the Ogwen valley. The narrow gauge Penrhyn Quarry Railway opened in 1801 to serve the Quarry connecting it with Port Penrhyn near Bangor and operated until 1962.

Bethesda has 40 Grade II listed buildings, including three pubs, in addition to the substantial and imposing Grade I listed Nonconformist Jerusalem Chapel. Noted for its number of chapels the town was named after the Bethesda Chapel, built in 1823 and the town subsequently developed around it.

Lake Ogwen

CAPEL CURIG

is at the very heart of the Snowdonia National Park. A rugged mountain village and a mecca for climbing and walking in Snowdonia. Capel Curig is the home of Plas-y-Brenin – the national centre for mountain activities. As with much of the rest of the British Isles, Capel Curig experiences a temperate maritime climate but is one of the wettest places in the UK.

Betws y Coed

BETWS Y COED

Swallow Falls

A very popular inland resort where the River Conwy meets its three tributaries flowing from the West. Much of it was built in Victorian times and it is one of the principal villages of the Snowdonia National Park. Set in a beautiful valley in the Snowdonia Forest Park, it is ideal for outdoor activity holidays. Numerous Craft and outdoor activity shops are in the village with the popular Swallow Falls nearby. The main street has numerous inns and bed-and-breakfast accommodation. A Museum with a miniature railway can be found at the railway station along with shops and restaurants. The 14th century church of St Michael's is one of the oldest in Wales and is worth viewing.

Thomas Telford's iron Waterloo Bridge built in 1815, which carries the A5 across the River Conwy, bears the cast iron inscription "This arch was constructed in the same year the battle of Waterloo was fought"

DOLWYDDELAN CASTLE on the A470, a few miles west of Betws-y-Coed, in a spectacular setting, must be the most dramatically sited castles in Wales.

Along the A5 is Ty Hyll (The Ugly House), named because of the huge uneven boulders in its walls.

Slate quarrying in FFESTINIOG is actually slate mining worked on the underground principle of alternate openings and walls or supporting pillars of solid slate. In this they differ from the workings in Penrhyn and Llanberis which are of the open kind consisting of a series of terraced steps. The dip of the slate veins at Ffestiniog necessitates the winning of the slate by burrowing below the surface in order to follow the course of the slate-producing strata which are as much as 1,500 ft. or more down. A unique feature of Ffestiniog slate is its resilience, which permits strips 1metre long or more, only 2mm. thick, being bent similar to a strip of steel. Apart from the manufacture of roofing slates, slate is widely used for billiard table beds, monumental purposes, brewery tanks, aquariums and pavements etc.

The slates were hauled by train on a narrow gauge railway laid in the early part of the 20th Century on a 2-ft. gauge track - at the time the pioneer of all narrow-gauge railways.

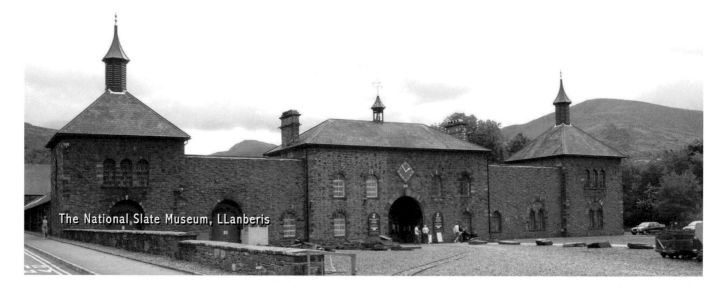

The National Slate Museum, LLanberis

DINORWIC QUARRY saw the first commercial attempts at slate mining in the late 18th Century. The business increased after the construction of a horse-drawn tramway to Port Dinorwic some years later. Towards the end of the 19th century when it was probably at its peak, some 100,000 tonnes was produced,

With the slate vein at Dinorwic being almost vertical and lying at or near the surface of the mountain, it allowed it to be worked in a series of galleries similar to that at the nearby Penrhyn quarry. The first quarrying was spread across some 16 sites and was a situation that lasted for many years.

The initial railway system brought transport problems as 5 quarries were all below the level of the railway and remained a problem for some 20 years when the lake level railway was built, the line of which is still evident today.

DINORWIG POWER STATION

The Dinorwig Power Station is a pumped-storage hydroelectric scheme, near Llanberis.

Construction began in 1974 and was completed 10 years later at a cost of £425m.

Dinorwig could store cheap energy produced at night by low marginal cost plant and then generate during times of peak demand, so displacing low efficiency plant during peak demand periods.

The scheme was constructed in the abandoned Dinorwic slate quarry. To preserve the natural beauty of Snowdonia National Park, the power station itself is located deep inside the Elidir Fawr mountain inside which there are tunnels and caverns. The power station is connected to the National Grid by underground cables to a local substation.

Water is stored at a high altitude at 636 metres in Marchlyn Mawr reservoir and is discharged through the turbines into Llyn Peris, over 500 metres lower, during times of peak electricity demand. It is pumped back up to Marchlyn Mawr during off-peak times. Although it uses more electricity to pump the water up than it generates on the way down, pumping is generally done at periods of low demand, when the energy is cheaper to consume.

The Snowdon Mountain Railway

Since 1896 visitors have been travelling to Llanberis, to experience this unique rail journey to the Summit of the highest mountain in Wales and England. Snowdon Mountain Railway has been described as one of the most wonderful railway journeys in the world with stunning scenery and awe-inspiring views.

BEDDGELERT

Once a busy port when the river was tidal and ships sailed all the way to the village centre before the building of "the Cob" by the coast.

Beddgelert (the grave of Gelert) village owes its fame to the story of Prince Llewelyn ap Iorwerth who decided on a hunting trip and left his infant son in the charge of his faithful dog Gelert. On his return, the Prince was greeted by Gelert, who noticed the dog's muzzle was soaked in blood, and his son nowhere to be seen. Llewelyn attacked the dog, and it fell to the ground gravely injured. However, he heard a cry from nearby bushes and found his son, safe in his cradle. Beside the cradle lay the body of a giant wolf covered with wounds, the result of a fight to the death with Gelert. It is thought that this story was made up by local traders some time ago in an attempt to lure Snowdon's visitors to their village! The tomb of Gelert supposedly stands in a beautiful meadow and consists of a slab lying on its side, and two upright stones. Experience the working environment of the Victorian miner in the Sygun Copper Mine on the outskirts of the village.

For one of the most scenic drives in the whole of Snowdonia, take the A498 which follows the course of the Glaslyn north-eastwards past two idyllic lakes - Llyn Dinas and Llyn Gwynant - before climbing up the Nant Gwynant Pass into the rocky heights of Snowdonia.

Lake Idwal

South Pembrokeshire

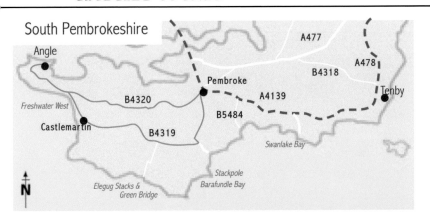

Barafundle Bay

Some of Pembrokeshire's Beauty Coastal Spots

Freshwater East Beach

Stackpole Quay

Elegug Stacks

Green Bridge

PLEASE NOTE the access road to Elegug Stacks and Green Bridge crosses MOD land and may be closed during Firing. Normal Firing Times are 09.00 - 16.30 for Day Firing: 18.30 - 23.30 for Night Firing. Check with the National Park on **0845 3457275** beforehand.

Gower Peninsula

The Gower peninsula -

Britain's first Area of Outstanding Natural Beauty is known for its coastline, popular with walkers and surfers. The southern coast consists of a series of small, rocky or sandy bays as well as larger beaches such as Port Eynon, Rhossili and Oxwich Bay. The north of the peninsula is home to the cockle-beds of Penclawdd. The interior is mainly farmland and common land. The Peninsula has many caves, including Paviland Cave and Minchin Hole Cave and has been the scene of several important archaeological discoveries. In 1823, archaeologists discovered a fairly complete Upper Paleolithic human male skeleton in Paviland Cave. This was the first human fossil to have been found anywhere in the world, and is still the oldest ceremonial burial anywhere in Western Europe. Gower is also home to standing stones from the Bronze Age. Of the nine stones eight remain today. One of the most notable of the stones is Arthur's stone [X] near Cefn Bryn. This was most likely carried by glacial ice from some distance away.

Castles on the Gower peninsula include:

Loughor Castle [1], Oystermouth Castle [2[, Oxwich Castle [3], Pennard Castle [4], Penrice Castle [5] and Weobley Castle [6].

Arthur's Stone

Pennard Castle

Rhossili Bay

Langland Bay

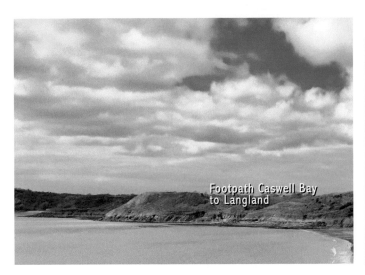

Footpath Caswell Bay
to Langland

Pobbles & Three Cliffs Bay

Mumbles Lighthouse

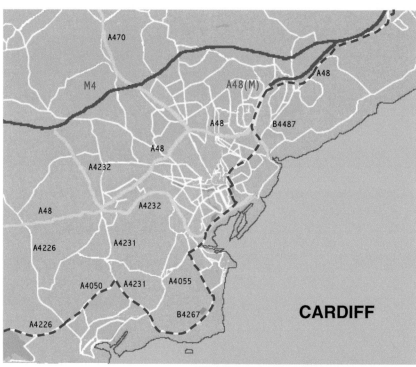

CARDIFF

Some buildings of interest in the City

1. Welsh Assembly Building (Y Senedd)
2. Wales Millennium Centre
3. City Hall
4. National Museum of Wales
5. Welsh National War Museum
6. Cardiff University
7. Pier Head Building
8. Cardiff Castle
9. Roath Park Lake Tower
10. Principality Stadium
11. Cardiff Barage

CARDIFF
Street Map

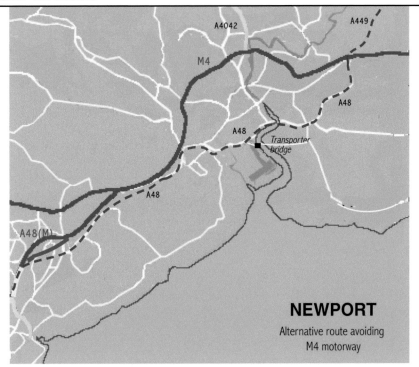

NEWPORT

Alternative route avoiding
M4 motorway

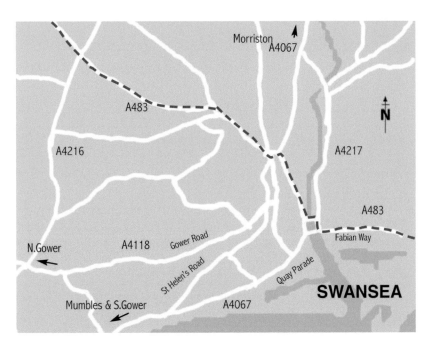

NOTES

Welsh - English Place Names
(in order on the Route)

Often used Welsh Words

Caerdydd	Cardiff
Casnewydd	Newport
Y Fenni	Abergavenny
Trefynwy	Monmouth
Crucywel	Crickhowell
Aberhonddu	Brecon
Llanfair-ym-Muallt	Builth Wells
Llandrindod	Llandrindod Wells
Y Drenewydd	Newtown
Y Trallwn	Welshpool
Wrecsam	Wrexham
Y Fflint	Flint
Bae Colwyn	Colwyn Bay
Ynys Mon	Anglesey
Porth Aethwy	Menai Bridge
Caergybi	Holyhead
Aberteifi	Cardigan
Abergwaun	Fishguard
Tyddewi	St Davids
Hwlffordd	Haverfordwest
Aberdaugleddau	Milford Haven
Penfro	Pembroke
Dinbych-y-Pysgod	Tenby
Caerfyrddin	Carmarthen
Porth Tywyn	Burry Port
Abertawe	Swansea
Y Gwyr	Gower
Y Bont Faen	Cowbridge
Barri	Barry

Aber	Mouth of (as of river)
Amser	Time
Araf	Slow
Arian	Money
Bara	Bread
Bore da	Good morning
Bwrdd	Table
Bws	Bus
Croeso	Welcome
Cwpan	Cup
Cymru	Wales
Da	Good
Dwr	Water
Ffon	Phone
Hiraeth	Longing
Iechyd da	Good health
Llaeth	Milk
Llan	A parish or settlement around a church
LLwy	Spoon
Maes Parcio	Car park
Modur	Car
Pob lwc	Good luck
Poeth	Hot
Pont	Bridge
Siop	Shop
Tocyn	Ticket
Ty Coffi	Coffee house
Yfed	Drink

INDEX

Printed in the United States
By Bookmasters